DATE DUE

DEC.   1994

A Tribute to
THE YOUNG AT HEART

BEVERLY CLEARY

By Julie Berg

Published by Abdo & Daughters, 4940 Viking Drive Suite 622, Edina, Minnesota 55435.

Library bound edition distributed by Rockbottom Books, Pentagon Tower, P.O. Box 36036, Minneapolis, Minnesota 55435.

Cover photo: Tom McDonough
Photo credits: People Magazine pgs. 17, 28
                University of Southern Mississippi pg. 26
                William Morrow and Co. pgs. 5, 19
                Special Collections Division-University of Washington Libraries pg. 8

Edited by Rosemary Wallner

LIBRARY OF CONGRESS CATALOGING-IN-PUBLICATION DATA
Berg, Julie.
     Beverly Cleary / written by Julie Berg.
          p.   cm. -- (Young at Heart)
     Includes bibliographical references and index.
     Summary: Presents the life of the author who created Ramona, Henry Huggins, Ribsy, and other well-know characters.
     ISBN 1-56239-222-0
     1. Cleary, Beverly -- Biography -- Juvenile literature. 2. Authors, American -- 20th century -- Biography -- Juvenile literature. [1. Cleary, Beverly. 2. Author, American.] I. Title. II. Series.
     PS3553.L3914Z59   1993
     813.54--dc20   93-12958
     [B]   CIP
                                                      AC

TABLE OF CONTENTS

A CHILDREN'S BOOK PIONEER

Beverly Cleary is perhaps the best-known writer of humorous, realistic fiction for young readers. A pioneer in writing about average American children and their world, Cleary transforms ordinary, everyday occurrences into hilarious incidents. She also writes in a style that is easy to read aloud or alone.

Whether she is writing believable fantasy or imaginative real-life stories, Cleary's remarkable attention to detail and vivid language has won her praises and awards from educators, librarians, and book critics. But the highest honor has come from the 25 awards she has won based on the votes of her 8- to 12-year-old readers.

"Writing for young readers was my childhood ambition," Cleary said. "However, when I write I do not think about writing for children. I write stories that I enjoy telling and feel that I am most fortunate that children enjoy reading them."

4

Beverly Cleary, children's book author.

LIFE ON THE FARM

Beverly (Bunn) Cleary was born on April 12, 1916, in McMinnville, Oregon. She lived with her mother, Mable, and father, Chester Lloyd, in a thirteen-room house on an eighty-acre farm in the Williamette Valley. Descendants of pioneers built the house. She spent her first six years happily playing alone there.

Her mother had a great influence on Cleary. Mable Bunn was an independent and determined woman who knew the importance of books, reading, and libraries. She established the first library in nearby Yamill. The library was located in an upstairs lodge room over a bank.

The room was filled with shabby leather-covered chairs and smelled of stale cigar smoke. There, Cleary made the most magic of discoveries. She found books for children!

But Cleary's carefree life was about to change. "Something had gone wrong with the pioneer dream of peace and plenty," Cleary said. "There was frightening adult talk of the World War, prices, interest rates, taxes, and mortgages. Then in the early 1920s came a year when a rich harvest did not bring in enough money to pay the debts and meet the needs of three people."

Cleary's parents did not have much money. They decided to rent their farm and move to the city. Young Cleary was excited about the move. At last she would have what she longed for: someone to play with and a big library full of books which she would learn to read.

The Suzzallo Library at the University of Washington, where Beverly
Cleary attended the School of Librarianship.

READING PROBLEMS

Cleary eagerly entered the first grade. But soon her joy turned into despair. School was not fun. And she had great difficulty learning to read.

"We had no bright beckoning book covers with such words as 'fun,' 'adventure,' or 'horizon' to tempt us on," she recalled. "No children played, no dogs romped, no ships sailed or planes flew on the covers of our schoolbooks. Our primer looked grim. Its olive-green cover with its black lettering bore the symbol of a beacon of light, presumably to guide us and to warn us of the dangers that lay within."

Cleary admitted that the sight of that olive-green cover still brings back the feelings of bewilderment she experienced that first year in school. In the city, she was confined to a classroom full of strange children after a life of freedom and isolation on a farm.

Her first-grade class was divided into three reading groups: Bluebirds (the best), Redbirds (average), and Blackbirds (the worst). Cleary was a Blackbird, the only girl in the group. She envied the bright, self-confident Bluebirds, who were mostly girls. They got to sit by the windows.

"Even the Redbirds in the center rows were better off than the Blackbirds," she said. "To be a Blackbird was to be disgraced. I wanted to read, but somehow I could not. I wept at home while my puzzled mother tried to drill me on the dreaded word charts. 'But reading is fun,' insisted mother. I stamped my feet and threw the book on the floor. Reading was not fun."

Cleary struggled along in her reading group. She was baffled when her group gathered in the circle of little chairs in front of the room to read over the phonic lists. The words meant nothing to her.

When she lost her place during a word drill, Cleary was sent to the cloakroom. There she stood in silence among the muddy boots and lunch bags that smelled of peanut butter. "Once the teacher [hit] my hands with a bamboo pointer with a metal tip for not paying attention," she said. "I was too ashamed to tell my parents."

Cleary found second grade more appealing. The teacher was kind and gentle. And there were no reading groups.

"I was able to plod through my reader a step or two ahead of disgrace," Cleary recalled. "But here another problem presented itself. Although I could read if I wanted to, I no longer wanted to. Reading was not fun. It was boring. Most of the stories were simplified versions of folktales that had been read aloud to me many times. There was no surprise left."

READING IS FUN

Then in the third grade, a "miracle" happened. It was a dull, rainy Sunday afternoon. There was nothing to do but thumb through two books from the Sunday-school library. After looking at the pictures, Cleary began to read *The Dutch Twins* by Lucy Fitch Perkins.

"Here was a book with a story in which something happened," Cleary recalled. "With rising elation, I read on. I read all afternoon and evening. By bedtime, I had read not only *The Dutch Twins* but *The Swiss Twins* as well. It was one of the most exciting days of my life. Shame and guilt dropped away from the ex-Blackbird who had at last taken wing. I could read and read with pleasure! Grown-ups were right after all. Reading was fun!"

From the third grade on, Cleary became an avid reader. Her school librarian suggested that Cleary should write children's books when she got older. Cleary was thrilled. "Of course," she said. "That's exactly what I wanted to do!"

By then, Cleary had moved beyond the Twin books. She was reading everything on the children's side of the library. She even developed a critical side. Why couldn't authors write about the sort of boys and girls who lived on her block, she wondered. Why couldn't authors skip all that tiresome description and write books in which something happened on every page? Why couldn't they make the stories funny?

The more she thought about those questions, the more she developed her own writing style. Her mother also gave her some good advice.

"My mother had important wisdom to impart," she recalled. " 'Reading is to the mind as exercise is to the body.' I was constantly directed to use my imagination and my ingenuity and to stand on my own two feet. When a teacher required a composition, my mother said, 'Always remember, the best writing is simple writing.' "

So at an early age, Beverly Cleary decided she wanted to write children's books. She had had enough of books about wealthy English children with nannies and pony carts. She also had had enough of books about poor children whose problems were solved by a long-lost rich relative who turned up in the last chapter. Cleary wanted to write funny stories about the sort of children she knew.

LEARNING TO WRITE

In 1938, Cleary attended the University of Washington School of Librarianship. "Not to catch a husband, as was the custom for young women of that time and place," she said, "but to become independent. I became a children's librarian, the next best thing to a writer."

As a librarian, Cleary met a variety of children. There were children of migratory workers, mill hands, doctors, lawyers, and "all the people who did whatever they could to survive during the Great Depression."

Two groups of children stood out. One was a band of unenthusiastic readers who came to the library once a week from a private school. They needed help in selecting books that might encourage them to read.

"They were a lively bunch and fun to work with," Cleary recalled. "But the sad truth was that there was very little in the library that they wanted to read. They wanted funny stories, and they wanted stories about the sort of children they knew. I sympathized because I had wanted funny stories about the sort of children I knew when I was their age."

The second group that often visited Cleary's library was the loyal story-hour audience. Although she told folktales and fairy tales, Cleary learned to write for children in those Saturday afternoon story hours.

In 1940, Cleary married Clarence T. Cleary. They moved to Oakland, California. During World War II, Cleary worked as a librarian at the Oakland Army Hospital.

After the war, the Clearys bought a house in the Berkeley Hills. Cleary found several reams of typing paper in a linen closet.

Beverly Cleary has always been involved with books.
She worked many years in a library before she began writing children's books.

"Now I'll have to write a book," she said to her husband. "Why don't you?" he responded. "Because we never have any sharp pencils," Cleary replied.

The next day, Clarence brought home a pencil sharpener. Cleary realized that if she was ever going to write a book, this was the time.

Shortly afterward, Cleary worked for three months in a large bookstore. She sold children's books during the Christmas rush. She saw all of the children's books published that year. This gave her a new view of children's books. Cleary was certain she could write a better book than the ones she read.

"After the Christmas rush," Cleary recalled, " I found myself for the first time in my life with free time, a quiet place in which to work and— oh joy!—confidence in myself."

HENRY HUGGINS

Cleary began her first story based on a real-life incident. Once she had seen two children take their dog home on a streetcar during a rainstorm. This turned into a story about a boy who would be allowed to keep a stray dog if he could sneak him home on a bus.

"When I finished that chapter," Cleary said, "I found I had ideas for another chapter. At the end of two months, I had a whole book about Henry Huggins and his dog Ribsy."

As she wrote, Cleary thought of the children she used to read to on the Saturday afternoon story hours. "When I began Henry Huggins," she said, "I did not know how to write a book. So I mentally told the stories to that remembered audience and wrote them down as I told them. This is why my first book is a collection of stories about a group of characters rather than a novel."

Beverly Cleary received many awards. The award
above was given to her by the University of
Southern Mississippi in 1982.

Henry Huggins was a composite of boys Cleary had known as a child. The story was named a Notable Book by the American Library Association.

As she continued to write, Cleary made another important discovery. She was able to find an inner voice, "the child within myself." That little girl prevented Cleary from writing down to children, and from poking fun at the characters. It also made her a better children's writer. For she was able to write her books as if she were a child. That made them more real and believable.

"We are collaborators who must agree," she said. "The feeling of being two ages at one time is delightful. One that surely must be a source of great pleasure to all writers of books enjoyed by children."

THE WRITING PROCESS

For Cleary, the most difficult part of writing is getting started. She thinks about a book long before she begins to write.

"It's much easier to not write than to write," she said. "So I usually chew pencils for a week, and swivel around in my chair a lot, and stare out the window, hoping to see some strange new bird so I can study it with my binoculars and go look it up in the bird book. Once I do get started, though, I keep at it."

Once she gets the first draft on paper, the fun begins. Then she can cross out, revise, and shape, which is her favorite part. "Every book has a trouble spot, though," she said. "When that happens, I've learned to put it out of my mind and turn to something else." The actual writing process takes about six months.

Several books about Henry and his friends were published. Then Cleary was invited to speak at a junior high school. Some girls asked Cleary why she didn't write stories for older girls. Cleary took their suggestion and wrote *Fifteen* (1956). She followed that book with *Jean and Johnny* (1959).

ADVICE TO BEGINNING WRITERS

Beverly Cleary has much experience in the world of children's books. She has made many mistakes, but has had many successes. Her first advice to aspiring children's book authors is to ignore all trends.

"Trends don't last," she said. "Original writers may start trends, if they write good, strong books."

She also tells beginning writers to write as though talking to a child. "An eight-year-old can understand anything you tell him," she said. "It's not necessary to have your stories look like telegrams. I have never changed a word to make it easier to read. If a child doesn't understand something, he can ask his parent, or use a dictionary. But most of the time, he can figure it out from the context of the story."

Most importantly, a writer must enjoy the work. "If I find that I'm not having fun with what I'm writing," she said, "I stop."

The most rewarding part of her career has been the number of people who tell of her positive influence over children. Because her books are fun to read, many children who didn't enjoy reading have found her books appealing, and have created better reading habits. That pleases Cleary.

"I remember the great feeling of release I got when I discovered I was reading," she recalled. "And enjoying what I read."

AWARD-WINNING BOOKS

Cleary's books have won many awards from educators, librarians, and book reviewers. In 1975, she won the American Library Association's Laura Ingalls Wilder Award. *Ramona and Her Father* was a Newbery Honor Book in 1978. In 1980, she won the Catholic Library Association's Regina Medal. *Ramona and Her Mother* won the American Book Award for children's fiction in paperback in 1981. *Ramona Quimby, Age 8* was a Newbery Honor Book in 1982.

The spunky Ramona Quimby first appeared in *Henry and Beezus* (1952). The character was so strong and likeable that Cleary decided to spin her off into her own series.

Ramona is one of Beverly Cleary's
most beloved characters.

Readers identify with Ramona's attempts to grow up gracefully while still retaining her spirited personality. The Ramona books have remained her most popular series.

Another important award came in 1984. That's when Cleary won the prestigious Newbery Medal for *Dear Mr. Henshaw.*

"*Dear Mr. Henshaw* was a most satisfying book to write," said Cleary. "It seemed almost to write itself. Because life is humorous, sorrowful, and filled with problems that have no solutions, my intent was to write about the feelings of a lonely boy and to avoid the genre of the problem novel."

Beverly Cleary's books appear in over ten countries in a variety of languages. Television programs based on Henry Huggins have appeared in Japan, Denmark, and Sweden.

Beverly Cleary's characters are much like children everywhere and her stories are lively and full of real-life situations. Beverly Cleary's books will be an enjoyment to generations to come.

A WRITER FOR ALL GENERATIONS

What makes Beverly Cleary's books so special is the details of their small-town settings. They also have lively dialogue and real characters who seem like family members. Cleary's unique gift for understanding the fears and joys of childhood have kept her books fresh. They will certainly be enjoyed by another generation of young readers looking for fun stories about children like themselves.

GLOSSARY

Draft -The first version of a manuscript.

Folktales -Traditional beliefs, practices, legends, and tales.

Great Depression - A time of hardship for Americans that began in October 1929 and lasted until 1939. During the Great Depression, many people could not find jobs and banks failed, leaving people with little money.

Manuscript -A book written by hand or typed. An author sends a manuscript to the publisher who makes it into a printed book.

Phonics - The study of sound; used in the teaching of reading.

Primer - An elementary textbook.

Ream - A quantity of paper, usually 500 sheets.

Trend - A direction of movement, usually with the latest fad or fashion.

World War I - A war fought from 1914 to 1918, in which Great Britain, France, Russia, Belgium, Italy, Japan, the United States, and other allies defeated Germany.

World War II - A war fought from 1939 to 1945, in which Great Britain, France, the Soviet Union, the United States, and other allies defeated Germany, Italy, and Japan.

INDEX